The Truth About
SOCIAL
MEDIA

PRIYANKA GULSHAN

Acknowledgement

In this book, an attempt has been made
to wake all the sleeping beauties
Who are are unaware of the direction
in which they are headed to !
You will see
and read in this book
what you want to see,
What you see no one will
What other's will you wont !
Because

" THE WAY
YOU
PERCEIVE THE WORLD
IS EXACTLY
HOW
YOUR WORLD
IS GOING TO LOOK LIKE ! "

INDEX

YOU LOST
THE GAME
WHEN
YOU
THOUGHT
OF PLAYING IT

AND NOW
YOU ARE NOT WHO YOU THINK YOU ARE
CZ YOU WERE
NOW YOU ARE JUST ANOTHER EMOTION PACKED IN
AND THE BEST PART
IS
THAT
YOU JUST DON'T KNOW IT '

An
Emoji

IT'S ALL ABOUT
YOUr

TIME

REALity

is

NOT

a LIE !

BEING SAD OR HAPPY
DOESN'T
MEAN THAT YOU SHOULD KNOW
WHAT YOU SHOULD
MAYBE THESE EMOTIONS ARE JUST TRYING TO REMIND YOU
OF BEING YOU '

YOU ARE THE TRUTH

CH 1 ATTENTION CONSUMERS

ALWAYS remember .....

" EVERYONE IS IN IT { period ! }
FOR SOMETHING ! "

You will have to ask
yourself :?

What is it, that you want ?

Not what you want,

But what you Really want ?

Your wishes may be granted
But you May never find those
Answers for which
You never looked for !

Don't rush for your answers,
Find the right questions first !

What will you do to grab someone's attention ?

Impress them

By Doing something for them by giving them exactly what they want, exactly the way they want to feel to be treated by an honest genuine person, by someone who really knows what he/she is doing, by decoding their emotions and using them in a way that they start liking you.

Mirror them

Just like a monkey, in-act what they are doing and then you are sorted, who doesn't like someone who knows how he/she feels, who knows what they are going through, people want someone who can relate to them !
Who can mimic them in a way they will never get offended but goal will be to make yourself reflect as their shadow who will never lie,
who speaks for itself,
has its own voice
But not having the real your voice at the same time.

By showing them their own face just like a mirror,
{even showing them their flaws but without pointing them out just like a mirror does, they will only see their own flaws if they will allow themselves to see or else even a mirror won't show them anything },
mirror their thinking,
their idealistic mirror of self,
because no one can ever hate himself/ herself, they will defend themselves at any cost, they won't let their own image down Even if 'you wear it' !
But even if they do not like themselves, still they will try to correct you because they hate themselves not you, they would like to make things right for you but not for themselves because the habit of being them won't let them be free, in any case you will have an upper hand !

Ignore them

Ignore and
The rest will happen .....
hurt their ego and soon you will find out that they want you badly in their life,
it's not a hidden fact as long as you are deprived of something you want that thing badly in your life but as soon as you have a

hold on it and it become usual to you then
the importance it had will loose it's
meaning !

*Give them the
importance they want*

Who doesn't want attention ?
Who doesn't want to be praised and loved ?
Everyone wants that !
But not forever,
because too much of anything looses it's
importance with time,
take your time,
Wait .
and then at the right time,
strike with the appreciation.

Relate to them

For real, if you have experienced what
they have gone through in their life,
instantly an invisible bond will be created
of trust, respect and feelings, that bond
would so pure that no one will ever be able
to break that,
because
Relate-Ability is the new thing !

But what if you are still unable to grab their attention, even after reading a number of books on human behaviour or psychology

What will you do then ?

Then you will take help from someone who knows what they are into and They know how to play the game, the people who have the experience which is required to play in that field,

But what if no one has ever played in the field you want them to play in,

What then ?

Then you will try to create someone who will know
how to .....

Maybe you will try to teach people, According to the requirements u want

But the main downside is that they can leave anytime, when they want to with your precious knowledge, they may have different views and opinions and could be biased and maybe untrustworthy too !

What will u do then ?

Then u will create the intelligence which
doesn't need someone's reliance ,
the one who is independent ?
and can work 24/7
without delay or excuses
or by being partial,
or by having thoughts ?
Or even thinking ?

Artificial think * King

A new concept or just a pirated version of
human, who is able and not, at the same
time, just like those pirated movies which
will allow you to see the story Cleary but
by being Blur at the same time !

Also the Name is quite opposite
of the required function

isn't ?
Or maybe we understood the requirements
wrong in the first place !

Yes, understood it wrong !
As usual .....

Well we moved into another conversation
but have you even noticed you just forgot
to ask what happened to the previous
question we started with
?

Because you were so involved with your
own question that what will happen next ?
For once you thought you had a choice,
But Those questions will still remain
Even if you will stop finding their answers
They will exist, no matter what !

Coming back to the question we started
this chapter with .....

Why would these awesome brain
manipulating / attention grabbing
techniques won't properly work ?

Another genius will reply
"No" that's not true I have used one of
these techniques in my real life
and they do work 100% !
"Yes", they do work but in Real life
Not in the new Digital / Reel life !
The Reel WORLD is quite different
from the Real World,

" It will never let you
Portray the REAL YOU ! "

And so the RULES for grasping Attention
will change according to their
FORMAT !
It Captures you !

Captivates you { keeps you locked it }

And will eventually own you forever !

REEL VS REAL
LIFE

Metaphorically as well as literally
And that's the actual Irony
By the end of this book probably you will
master 'figure of speech' abstractly !

In Reel life you don't know the person,
you don't know what they are hiding, and
why they are hiding it,
they could be pretending being someone or
acting like some,
Artificial intelligence would never be able
to catch their real faces,
Even If they will stop monitoring your
time and staring monitoring your feelings
behind those posts, which they do now,
those emojis you use won't help,

" You May Never Know
what that smile withholds "

they still won't be able to exactly tell The
Cause, their behaviour and its accurate
meaning !

" because
You Can Hide,
but you really don't have
much of a choice
for a hideout ! "

Then hiding would for surely defy the
whole purpose of it being in existence,
but you can still try,
Hope is the way out,
just to figure out one day
that it won't work , not until you let it !

Because in the end it's not about the post
or the content whether you watch
a conspiracy theory or
real news or some interviews or
some people do make stupid videos or
take sides in order to be known,
in Order to be seen,
But in the End,
The only Goal is .....

To destroy someone else's time Right ?

Destroy time ?

why not use this term from now on,
instead of the usual 'Waste time'
Right ?

We are not Evolving
The theories you are used to that
technology will make us work for it
in the future is not the future

It iS Now !

11

It's quite ironic how they show technology
ruling over humans in sci-fi movies

" It doesn't need
to dictate,
If you are willing
to make it rule ! "

Isn't ?

You are not Apart
Even if you make conspiracy theories
You are A Part of this System !

And maybe A prominent ONE !

And you can't even Deny it !
If it wasn't for the technology/
if this technology wasn't there then people
would have never even known your
conspiracy, or news or the shows you like !

Everyone and I meant it !

You work
for this technology Everyday !

You post, tag,
make statements every day
You are working for a platform,
Which is in the air,

By BEING in THE WEB !
All The TIME !
You work to grow your platform
Provide them so much value to eventually
Connect everyone to the internet
isn't ?

" you need this Technology as much as it Needs You ! "

In the end what counts is the time you are
allowing yourself to spend,
the precious time which you are willing to
Sacrifice by Your Will !

Did you forget the point again ?

Or not ?

Did your forgot to ask about the question
which we were discussing previously ?

If you didn't forget then you are awesome
But if you did then we will figure a way out
by the end of this book to make you Think
the way you should !

coming back to the point .....

what would Grab Attention ?

If The Aim :
is to consume as much time as possible
At any cost or else you would loose the job
{ and it is more of a loss for them than
you loosing your job because you don't
realise the power of time and until you do
you will never get it }
since the company would pretend to go
bankrupt, the usual story,
you know the drill,
but if you don't
then No One Can Help You !

These are the ways in which
They really grab Your
Attention .....

* Automatically *

If you already have enough followers or
because these people are following you
from a long time, then sometimes even if
you move a finger you will be noticed
because by that time you will get a trusted
audience, those people who will believe
you no matter what happens,
they will support you and will watch you,
you can also call this as an
' Involuntary Habit '
if someone is used to of doing something,

In this case watching a particular person's videos, its really hard to break away from that habit, but it's not Impossible,
If you stop watching their content due to any reason, or Your Frequency of watching them decreased for that particular person then
In An addicts Language
As your daily dose will decrease
You will heal and your addiction won't even last long but for this to happen you must not be manipulated by other,
For e.g. you may stop watching a specific persons content but it is possible you replaced watching their content with someone else,

" its just like moving out of a Trap just to land in Another ! "

which will result in your addiction being renewed just as your curiosity for that particular person. But if you overcome the main reason, the main addiction of consuming things continuously on your own, only then will You be able to become free from that bond, this may also happen if you start disliking their content, due to difference of opinion, In case your opinions Won't Match, or if they start giving their attention to the things in which you are not interested in, or this may even happen

even if they ignore you or start giving time
to other people, or maybe this may also
occur if they, themselves start uploading
less videos or in other words less frequent
uploads, which is why every platform
insists on uploading frequently and
regularly, so that they keep a hold on your
attention,
because it's a loss for both the sides,
people may lose their tiny money but the
company may loose their customer forever
to another platform, which they can't
afford even if the Cost Demands removing
some of their own.

Fight

by making different opinions from the rest
of the world, that is by Challenging
everyone's views, this will eventually force
everyone to stay either to fight with them
or to bash them or to troll them as they
say

' Any kind of publicity is
Good publicity '

It's the same thinking they use that
by hook or crook
work should be done !

Even Acharya Chanakya said that !
I have also written books inspired by
acharya you can check those out in case,
Yes you are right I am promoting
But why don't everyone check out or
watch there reviews or promotion videos
Despite of the fact them being famous,
People don't because they don't care
But remember the first line of this chapter
Everyone's in it for something
They will even watch those reviews which
are out of their usual category, from what
they watch regularly, something different
from what they are used to,
if there is something in it for them, "yes"
I know you can guess
It's coming in your mind,
You are getting there.....   Rewards !

Greed

See how quickly you got offended with this
word " greed ", isn't ?
Rewards sounded much better,
You just got offended just as we discussed
above in the previous point
{ They will get the attention they want by
provoking or irritating you - Don't Look
only from your your own perspective,
try to look from other person's too }
Because that is the only way out !

Don't worry I will just keep irritating you
So that you can learn, throughout this
book
If you really want to learn then you must
question and for that you must be aware,
So don't just mug up , be aware and then
read !
In case you are wondering, someone will
always be there to differ, lets say that
someone will say that - I didn't get
offended, you didn't genius because your
subconscious already read what was
coming ahead,
but your conscious was focused and so
congrats on being highly focused but you
will need to be careful about your
subconscious catching and picking up on
things unconsciously,
this just doesn't happens with you it
Happens With Everyone,
the only Solution to this is
that you can't prevent yourself from
seeing thing and going into your
subconscious but you can surely
Limit
them you can make sure that you don't go
there where there is no need for you to go,
the point is
            Don't 'see what you are
                not meant to see',
but some genius would usually
say that .....

" it's difficult, but if it wouldn't,
then surely it won't be the Solution
you were Searching for ! "

Did you again forgot the point what we
were talking about ?
I bet You did. This time .....
Not everyone is greedy but who doesn't
like some free gifts, rewards are actually
quite different from greed, the hunger for
greed will never stop, if someone is greedy
they would not want anything and
everything But only their required desires
unlimitedly, but if someone wants a gift or
a reward, is quite in the human nature
that they will also look for a praise,

" what's even a Reward Means,
if it's given without Praise ! "

Right ?
These rewards,
gifts will lure them into temptation for
watching the required content in order to
be eligible for participating, they would
either ask a question from the content
they have created or so on you know it,
but the point is give away's and this stuff
for sure works in grabbing your attention,
your time which they demand actually !

19

Expectations / Feelings

You have to always remember everyone
who follows another person in the reel
world they are in a Digital Relationship,
In which one expects one type of content
or information from the other and that is
the only pure bond between them
if that breaks that is
when you upset someone they gets
annoyed they might leave you but they
can't if they have been with you from a
long time, instead they will listen to you in
order to either point you out or to correct
you, same is the case in the reel world
people will either comment and explain
them their mistakes or troll those people
they follow, think of this, like this, if you
hate someone but you still follow them to
see their posts, their progress only in
order to point out their mistakes or you
following your x's account in order to see
what they are doing in their life, even if
you have moved on,

" that feeling, to know.ing what
happens will always keep You
hooked and Connected ! "

and this point is also connected to Yet
Different from the next point .....

20

by Triggering their Curiosity

what will happen next ?
what do think is going to happen
tomorrow ?
they will leave you guessing / make you
wait and just when your patience will be
about to give up then they will release the
content and this is the secret recipe of a
viral content, there you go
I just revealed the most important secret
of any creators life,
Now go and work for the internet !
Haha ..... :)
You will one day
A Lame Joke ?
Maybe, hmm .....
we will see if that remains a joke only.
No one knows what the future beholds ?

if They Support YOU

If they name you, for example shoutouts
or mentions or even when they involve
you, or interact with you,
just like they way I am talking to you,
with the help of this book, you were
involved in this book from the start and I
am sure you will evolve after you finish
reading this book, not from a monkey
but knowledgeably.

sometimes accepting someone's point of view maybe by questioning them and finding out the real things yourself will all it will take for you to discover the truth, but

" You Won't See Anything 'if you wont allow yourself to' "

It will always be up to you !
The world revolves but your world will revolve around you and so For your World To let you Tell The Truth 'You Must Abide your own Rules' !
Coming back to the point .....
Involvement leads to a connection, a bond, for example if something is about you, or for your own good, you won't ever deny to listen to it, as we know everyone's in it for something, but for you to find the the thing you are looking for You Must Look First, sitting back on that couch watching continuously eating frozen won't help,
And so before you read the next chapter make sure you do something for you self, for example start by writing your goals and dream on a sheet,
"Prepare For The Future 'before you learn the hard way' !"   See you There !
Not every thing is a conspiracy ?
Only if lamest-east was a word ! :)

CH 2   WHAT DO YOU WANT TO FEEL TODAY ?

YOUr happiness is Being Loaded .....

Wait for your customised feed .....

Loading .....

```
                 HOW ARE YOU FEELING TODAY ?
                 HERE'S YOUR FEED FOR TODAY-
                     THIS FEED WILL FEED YOU
                 WITH ALL THE UNWANTED STUFF
           THAT WILL LEAD YOU NOWHERE IN YOUR LIFE .
          AND THEN ULTIMATELY IT WILL CONSUME YOU
                          TO A POINT
                   THAT YOU WILL REALIZE
           WHAT YOU HAVE LOST WAS TOO PRECIOUS !
                          BUT THEN
             YOU WILL BE SO BROKE BY THAT TIME
          THAT YOU WONT THINK OF COMING OUT OF IT
   BUT YOU WOULD EVENTUALLY THINK OF PRODUCING MORE OF IT
           IN HOPE OF GETTING MORE OF WHAT YOU WANT
                 WHICH YOU DON'T REALLY KNOW
                     AND NEVER WILL .
                      BUT FOR SURE
           YOU WILL BE EVENTUALLY LOST FOREVER
           IN THIS VICIOUSLY CYCLE OF DEBT TRAP !
                   ENJOY YOUR DAY !
```

" Feed "

What do you understand by this term ?
I am sure of what I do understand by this
because of it being correctly named
It means to me as if we are being prepared
to consume
- our feed,
- our needs,
- desires,
to watch, to see a particular type of
content , our needs are being fulfilled, just
so that we will fulfil their needs,
They have created that feed so that
someone could consume it, give their time
to it so that they can have it period !

because nothing is for free, everything has
it's own price even if it doesn't accept they
form of payment you use,
BARTER system remember ?
Exchange of a good with another
Just so both can live happily ever after, ?
Which is not the case always ! Maybe ?

Their need is to capture as much time as
they can from us, take as much time as
they can from us and for this They don't
Have to Plan too much because there are
people like you only who have been
employed,
but you still can't blame anyone
because it won't be right to do so,

Since you are moving each step ahead
with your own consent, my goal by writing
this is not to blame anyone but to create
awareness that we should be more
particular in what we want or
else we will loose all our time in those
stupid cat videos.

The point is when you go to learn how to
swim you Don't Go directly to the ocean
and dive in, that way you won't even
Survive !

To survive you must Practice !

You must Know Everything before just
diving in, you won't prepare for the Worst
In this Way but you will be in it,
don't think that You Can Overcome those
fears By Facing Them in the first go,
Go practice !

• First you stay away

• Then you practice and try

• And only then will you be prepared
  to face the ocean

This is the Ultimate Solution !
{not the only One} :)

25

So you must

- stay away from that content,

- try to overlooking the things you are used to see, your curiosity rushes you to see, try reducing that and only then by practice will you be able to master the art of being aware and will be able to choose the way you want to, to see the right things which are meant for you,

- Try to practice your own will , Try to See what you actually would have chosen by your own will not by someone's recommendation,

- Don't allow them to feed you, if you are there by your own will, then make your will happen, don't let anyone hinder your goals or perspectives or point of views !

But as we know some genius will still be there to think and differ and point out saying .....
We still have a choice !
We are free !

If you really were, then go and see your history on the web out of your 10 last thing you searched or saw, notice end

point out how many of them were really
useful to you,
I doubt you genius,
not even a single one would be !
Genius being genius will say
No a single one was useful !
My reply to you is that : =
It's not really About The Frequency
But

'it's about the choices we make everyday'
Even if someone would have searched 9
things right which were useful to them still
The point will always remain the same and
that is .....

Even if there is still that 1 thing you
searched involuntarily that is consuming
your time, and that is the whole point,

" even if You Are Entangled
by the thinest string in the world,
You Are still Being Held Capitative
in your own prison
Which You Have Created for Yourself
the perception of having a choice
is NOt a Choice ! "

You can choose what you want to
See everyone is free
Or at least they think they are .....

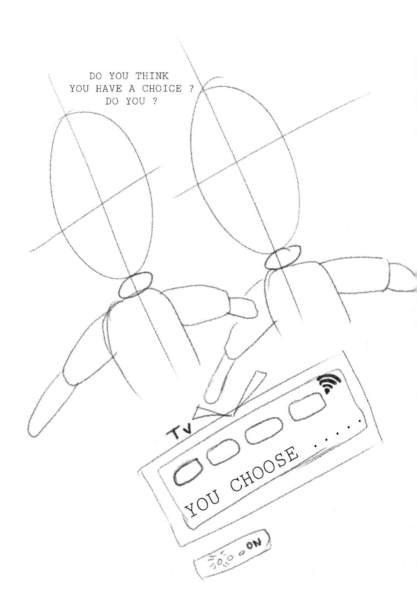

DO YOU THINK
YOU HAVE A CHOICE ?
DO YOU ?

" the Illusion of Choice "

You think you really have a choice ?

PAY your Attention !
and
Choose .....

there is a store
you can go left or right
choose ?
if you go right then go left ,
or else keep going to were you were
headed.
what do u think now ?

" choice is a perception designed
to make you think that You Are in control,
even when you are Not ! "

You pay your attention in exchange for the
content you consume, you have a choice to
pay your money, to consume the same
content without ads, you have a choice to
decide where to watch, what to watch,

" but do you have a choice
to Choose Not To Watch At All ?
'yes', you do !
but the question is Will You ? "

What is your free pass time ?
What do you do everyday nowadays all the
time ?
We know the answer and it won't differ
drastically for most of you !

The perception of having a choice,
Means that you will have to choose,
Without having a real choice,
You can choose to stay in place a or b
But you don't have a choice to quit,
Why ?
Because you want to stay
You have a option but you won't
consider it
To even consider it
You will have to break free
because no one is to blame for this
You are not in a prison
But you are a prisoner of
Your own
You Lost Your own Rights to choose
Long Ago,
This is not you,
not your will,
But someone else's !

have you ever seen any addict ever ?
if you haven't let me tell you this
They Would Go to any Extinct !
to get what they want,

" Because as humans you
can control your demands but when
Your Demands Control You,
then you are no longer
termed as human "

When this happens then you take form of
those uncontrolled feelings those emotions
which dominates you and they won't even
let you be you,

When this synthetic stuff is inside you,
your natural processes starts questioning
their existence, your body starts
deteriorating,

But
There is a way even to save those addicts
But it will only work if they want it to work
Only if they want to live and are strong
enough, are willing to let go of their
perception, their previous mindset, of
what they used to think, some of them also
think that they deserve pain which is why
they use these substances, these synthetic
feeling { synthetic emotions } to make
them feel that pain,

31

To be allowed to think what you are used to think of yourself, it's high time to change that, If you know your mistakes, then that realisation is the only thing which will guide you in the future and will prevent you from doing something stupid again, you don't need to punish yourself, for what has happened instead Be Read for what is about to happen.

I m not just talking about some substance but also about those feeling those emotions which you crave everyday,

Even if you are used to those sad songs which your heart wants, in case you just had a breakup that song you choose will provide you with that pain, without it you won't really feel that pain but you will Feel the Nothingness, the emptiness which no one wants to feel !

But Why ?

because of being scared of their trust self, they want to hide forever in those synthetic feeling, but in reality hiding won't help, you will have to Face that Nothingness one day and when that happens you will realise that no matter what you do your true self is different, that silence will show you your reality, only if you will allow yourself to see it !

Some people desire sadness some happiness, they dance so much that they end up breaking something, those uncontrollable awesome people, are everywhere even around us, some people break things because of being happy and some do that in a rage, when these synthetic feelings overtake your real feeling this is the result of that !

Everyone is different but the point is that whatever you feel through what ever medium, you feel it because you believe thats your reality it can be music, movies, watching or doing something, but deep inside your heart you will know that those feeling aren't really real, they are not your true feeling !

Some people even mimic feeling of having some feelings for people, exactly the same way in which they mimic those emotions you do to involuntary, don't be surprised this is called being influenced, and

" It's Done
even before you know it ! "

You won't even realise what happened because You Thought since you were doing these things voluntarily, so you thought them but

'No', there is a high possibility
that Someone's Thought That For You !

You got influenced, when your
subconscious herd that thing or saw it,
your conscience sry conscious it :)
won't it realise it
But your subconscious will,
I will give you an example, this will prove
right only if you do the exact way as I am
telling you or some may have even
experienced it, but those will be very Few
who actually Noticed It,

* *Very Important* *
" Eyes of the Subconscious "

Go to any video platform watch only a
single video, don't watch anything except
that video that day and don't try to look
any below that video or above that and
after watching it click the screenshot of
your recommendations, basically of that
page where you saw that video but without
noticing those videos consciously or
reading anything or seeing anything, you
can take the help of your friends to click
that screenshot or if you know about your
phone enough its actually quite easy, it's
different for every phone though
sometimes you have to click to power and
home or assistant menu or so one, search

for your device how to click a screenshot
learn that in a way that you won't have to
look at the page too click a screenshot

and then { clearly mentioned in points }

- after watching an entire video
  consciously but without looking anything
  on that page
- click the screenshot like you have
  practiced without looking at anything
  else
- then close that app don't open it again
  and
- just talk or have a normal conversation
  or a discussion with your friends
- then after finishing your conversation go
  back to those screenshots you have
  captured earlier and you will see the
  magic
- There is no magic in reality, you will see
  what you talked about with your friends
  was related to one of those
  recommendations or suggestion from
  that screenshots which you have capture
  earlier !

I am sure that you will find those topic to
be quite similar to what you have
discussed, your opinions while talking
about those topics may differ,
But thats not the point,
the point is .....

That what ever your subconscious saw or heard, it started working on it instantly, you opinions may get changed with the help of your conscious but those main ideas those topics of discussions those heading would be same of what your subconscious saw in those screenshots,

I know this is quite difficult to do, not to look but to click screenshots, but I have been there, done that, many times just to see how our subconscious reacts to external things, don't just take my word for it, I want you to do that yourself, some things are better learned if experienced,

This littel experience will not only teach you how to try to discover,
But will also show you the reality of you, that most of the things your are thinking right now, you just herd them anywhere near you or just saw them but you didn't noticed them consciously but your subconscious did and so it acted accordingly,

Humans are far more intelligent than technology, they created it, don't underestimate yourself once you start finding the truth, there is no going back you will be able to see through the real you

and will be able to tell what's you and
what's not you !

This is the reality of your subconscious !

But then
what is the reality of your conscious ?

What is really real is that nothingness
which we have talked about earlier which
you just keep ignoring and so just for once,
for yourself try being silent doing nothing
just for 5 minutes and you will realise your
true self, the one you never looked at,
realise your existence, your potential, that
silence will teach you, make you realise
your capabilities, your abilities !
Your true power lies within you,
you have the potential to change the
world, all you have to do is trust yourself !
Only then will you be able to do what you
want to, to break free from the trap you
have kept yourself in from so long !
Even from the restrictions of judgements
imposed on you by your subconscious
if any were there, Because somethings can
only be experienced not taught and so at
the end of the day .....

" If You Don't Really want what you
Desire for You Won't Get It ! "

because

"no One Can Help Those who
don't want to be helped"

You will have to help yourself first,
if you want to get out,
there is no other way !!!

Coming back to .....
" Synthetic Emotions " and their effects

Is this term only valid for those who do
stuff or mimic emotions voluntarily or
involuntarily as we discussed it before or
is it valid for any other thing also ?

It is valid for everything, for everything
which gives you a feel of the feeling you
want,

Read ahead carefully !

just like when you fake an emotion,
an expression, an experience,
You body Shows it in the form of
" Body Leakage "

That is when a person is lying for a few
statement's he/she will look in a certain
direction and when is speaking the truth
they will look in a different direction,

weather someone is speaking the truth or not it can be determined by a lot of things, expressions and techniques but the point is when you are lying, even if the person standing in front of you, even if he/she is unable to find out the truth but You Will Always Know, your body will always know the truth, no matter what !

" You Can Lie to everyone, but not To Yourself "

Similar in the case of synthetic emotions even if you borrow the feeling from an outer source you heart will know it's not the true real feeling that it really desires for !

Since we have already discussed synthetic emotions and about Consciousness topic's in details now is the time to Merge them .....

How Exactly will your conscious and subconscious will react to theses synthetic emotions ?

These emotions are fake your heart knows it but your brain doesn't even if you acquire these emotions consciously by will by watching some content or by ignoring

some content it will have an effect on you
wether you like it or not !

For example, one may watch something
sad by his own will to feel those fake
synthetic emotions { That's fine }

But

one who has been shown some sad ads
may ignore them even if he/she ignores
them consciously,
or may not even notice them consciously
but notice them subconsciously,
Still either way your brain saw those ads
wether you noticed it or not,
and those ads will eventually give you that
synthetic feel of sadness even if you don't
want it, it's not some Proven Fact but you
can't just prove everything you have to
experience things,

So what's the Solution ?

I Haven't Come Up With One; because I
really don't think we have one here, my
experience which I shared with you
" eyes of the subconscious " is extremely
original and I am sure you will not find this
anywhere but that's the whole point
originality takes time and its also open for
being corrected or being improved or

40

evolved into something more than what it was earlier

And so as of now I haven't found any solution to escape these synthetic emotions even if your subconscious took it unwilling but for the future I hope If I notice enough who know maybe I will find something or even you can,

No one knows what The Future beholds but this is for sure it does Contains

'The possibilities of the UNKNOWN !'
:)

Lame ?

'No', now its getting Real !

Define Reality ?

What you see or feel or experience but you won't consider it real until you yourself won't believe or experience it and so I have to make thins lame just so that they don't sound real ?

And there you go .....

Now it's Lame ! ;)

" Dopamine "

You may feel good for sometime by
relishing this hormone by spending your
time on the net but as soon as you will
come in the reality you will realise that
you have actually done nothing in order to
feel good, everything is still the same,
you may have watched workout videos
and would have thought to do the same,
But you just felt so good in staying lazy
and seeing them do what you want to and
you knew that you could improve but still
you did nothing about it !

" you will get no where
if You won't Make A Move "

and those true feeling you are Hiding,
taking Shelter from this Reel world
lit by An LED SCREEN this May Save You,
may help you overcome your emotions for
sometime
but your true feelings won't go anywhere
they will still be there just to remind you
that you will have to work hard on
yourself in order to do what you really
want to do, that you will have to leave this
instant gratification in order to really
achieve something which is useful and
which really have a meaning,
which is worth spending time for

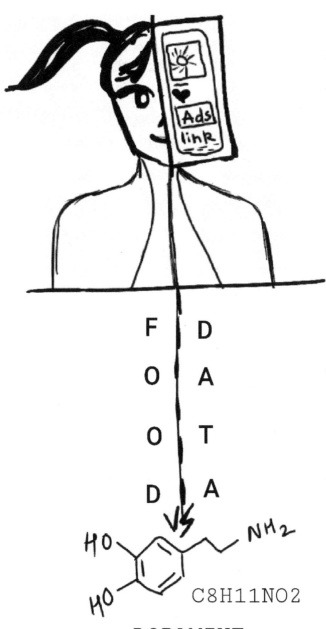

F   D

O   A

O   T

D   A

$C_8H_{11}NO_2$

DOPAMINE

But for this the first step is acceptance, you will have to accept first that whatever you have done till now has wasted your time, take your time, don't accept because I am saying so accept when you really feel what you have done, only then will you be able to move forward, after realising and truly accepting, with the help of your will power and your sheer determination, if it is true enough then they both will guide you the way out, 'it is the true path which will lead you out of this addictive nation', but in order to do so you must be willing to, no One Will Come To hold your hand and Grab You from your collar out of this mess, you have kept your foot there with your Consent And so your consent is a must if you Really want to lEave this Fake reeL WORLD !

"Yes", you have a choice. Here !

How is this a really choice ?
because it has not been created by someone, no one has designed this choice but you and even the way out may be different for everyone because

" when You Are The prisoner
of your own prison then
only you will decide your Way Out ! "

CH 3 CURIOSITY DRIVES IN

What a curious animal human is ?

curious and an animal
The two thing when mixed together can
lead to either a grand success or a mass
dose of failure, it depend, on what you will
do with your power to think and act
Will you be human or inhuman ?

You will always have a choice ?
But sometimes our decisions are
pre - decided too,

Actually we don't really choose !
But our circumstances does,
what we have been through in our life,
those instances make your choices and
they make us move as they want us to
And even if your human side kicks in,
your experience will always be there to
remind you to choose differently

Can curiosity be driven by the wrong
perception ?

Why not ?

What you see is what you speak
what you speak is what you think .....

But what happens,
If it's not what you thought then you will
be termed as the unpredictables
or the humans

the best part of being unpredictable is that
you are never accountable to anyone
because you simply don't care !

now imagine some artificial program being
in the right hands,
Lets suppose in your hands
what will u do
first stalk your x
or what do normal people do ?
can't think of any i just don't do these
things see everyone has their own
preferences
maybe i would just let it be
but one may stalk the people they like
or fix their agendas
others could do something to promote
themselves while we can only think of the
good possibilities
there are bad people too
what would bad people do ?
something bad obviously and they would
do that openly,
because being bad is more fun when you
show them you real side

But

There is another category the CRZY1S
who think they are doing the right thing ,
because they don't have a choice !

what is a choice ?
an illusion depicted in such a way that 'it
compels a person to choose',
like they had a choice in the first place

What is so special about these CRZY1S ?
they think systematically !
more predictable than the normal beings
and they are good convincers/speakers
too mostly
Way more organised that you and I will
ever will be
And defiantly have a privilege of knowing
the things we don't

What would you do if you see them
in person some day ?
there is no need to do anything
they will
Just simply tell you
what they want you to do
Good convincers remember .

Some genius will always be there and will
say they are extraordinary!

But

Even acharya Chanakya once said that

" No person is extraordinary. But when an
ordinary person gets caught in
extraordinary circumstances. So while
solving them That ordinary person also
looks extraordinary. "

What is Reality ?
The way you perceive thing is real for you
What is real for you,
It may not be the real thing for others,
On the bases of what they see,
What they have been taught
from their childhood,
they believe it,
To such an Extinct,
That the meaning of life for them is to fulfil
that purpose,
Without that purpose,
There is no meaning to their life,
Without that purpose,
In which they believe in,
it's the end of the world for them,

While you can thing the CRZY1S are being
bad, bad people are already bad and those
who have been raised good some of them
might have an agenda of their own,
will they turn bad or not ?
It's not for sure but the point is When
Everyone Turns Bad,

Then what happens ?

" Bad becomes the new normal "

Will then this fight continue ?
Of course it will be continued .....
But
The only choice you will have by then will
be to choose between,

a Devil or an Evil ?

What will you choose ?
the bad
or
the worse,
Both sides are so badly rusted
They can't even help themselves
All anyone on both the sides
can think of is of themselves !

When humanity is out of the question and
you can't stand the sight of the fight
What will you do then ?
Will you Leave ?
Will you retreat ?
Or will you accept your defeat !

Now Choose !

You have a hell lot of options to choose
from !   { See you still have a choice ! ! ! }
But it's just another predictable one !

THE WAY YOU
PERCEIVE THE WORLD
IS EXACTLY
HOW YOUR WORLD
IS GONNA LOOK LIKE !

DONT THINK FROM YOUR BRAIN !
DON'T JUDGE ON THE BASIS OF WHAT YOU SEE OR ARE SHOWN
THINK FROM YOUR HEART !
IT'S ALREADY IN SYNC WITH HUMANITY.

" THE PERCEPTION "

How you perceive the world
is how it's going to look like to you,
If someone wants a fight
he/she will find a fight,
If someone want peace,
he/she will find peace,
Under any circumstances,
under any situation,
our brains are capable enough
to find us what we want,
Making that purpose live at any cost,
if it's the main goal then even a normal
walking lady could like a fighter
to someone who wants a fight !

Which side are you on ?

What purpose do you have ?

Why is it so important for you to have an
agenda, To live like a human, why ?

why can't you people Have Peace ?

Clearly they want to save their own
purpose,
they live because of it,
if everyone gets peace maybe they will just
die aimlessly,
What a curious animal human is .
Right ?

51

Since you understood
The Depths
of how humans think in a dramatic way,
now is the time
to come back to the point .....

In the REEL world
This perception plays a huge role,
In the real world
The world is same
But just like everyone
thinks differently
and sees things different,
in the way they want to see those things,
similarly in Order for this REEL world
to be successful they had to make it as
much as real as possible

BUT HOW ?

Through personalised feeds
and recommendations,

- By showing you what you want to see
  and
- by leaving out every other possibility
  that differs your opinion
we will talk more about in CH - 6 of this
book as well as In Part - 2 of The Truth
about Social media

"Yes", I just said it, part-2 will be there !

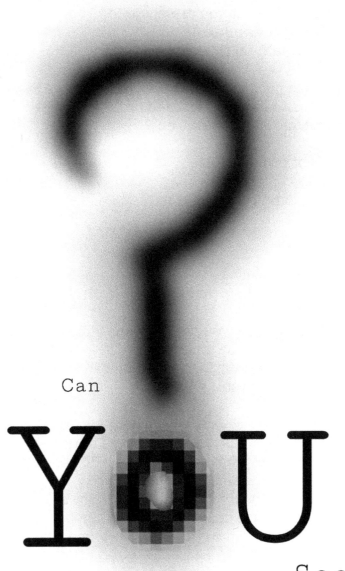

Can Y O U See

"YES", you can see,
but only what you are made to,
what you want to,
not what you should see,

In the perfect REAL world we will have to
listen to both the sides in order to decide
on which side are we on ?

Right or Left ?

It Doesn't really Matter !

Does it ?

Those who still don't get it
Sry I can't help you !

If any genius would say he/she will choose
the 3 rd side or create one
I would ask him/her not to read
But to understand !

Every writer plays with words
But sometimes those words are meant to
show what you are doing, some do it boldly
they get banned, some people do it
subconsciously by depicting a story and
some like me does it all differently, by
saying and not saying it at the same time,

Coming back to the point .....

They won't let you listen to both the sides
in the REEL world like you had to listen in
the REAL world,

because then that will defy the whole
purpose of their existence,

that would not let them complete their
task of obtaining the target level of time
which is needed to be achieved,
From you,
From your precious life,

Which maybe you don't think really is
precious, probably that's why you were
wasting it, Giving it up for cat videos.

But you will eventually know the
importance of life,
once you will loose the time which you
needed the most,
Everyone has their own realisation,
It depend on you wisdom teeth
Yes it depends on the fact that
how old are you ? :)
Age does forces a person to think
differently,
the 20 years old version of you will be
much more stupider than the wiser 36
year older version of you will be,
Wait for it,
You will eventually notice it !

" Lying without Body Leakage "

How do people actually lie ?

The CRZY1S
How ?

Why their face or their body don't show
any sign of body leakage ?

Why no one can prove anything against
them, why are the so perfect ?

This is How they do it :)

{ *this may include but is not
limited* }

I.   You don't have to lie, you have to
believe that lie, if you won't
believe them then your body will
show them { body leakage }

II. Why are they so perfect at it ? No
one is but when they don't have a
choice its usually do or die

III.   In the ocean of truth mix the drops of of those lies you though and they will hide themselves

IV.   Say what they want to hear, not what you want to say .

V.   Be relatable, it's the best cover up !

VI.   Don't just look at people like people look at them like personalities and then bit by bit, layer by layer understand them, give them what they want

VII. Observe every detail, in order to Lie one must be a good observer because most of the times when you are unable to come up with something your surroundings still can save you ! Just observe !

VIII. You looked at the situation it's fine but now go again and take a better look

IX. Once you start lying and know everything then you will eventually understand how you can never trust anyone and so you must have those people in your life on whom you can blindly rely on, life is not a game to be played alone

X. You must know your opponents strengths and weaknesses along with your similarities with them

XI. Breathe don't get nervous, as long as you breathe and be calm you won't get caught

XII. Don't worry about the other
person blaming you, focus on
your self, your words

XIII. Lastly if you think you can lie
perfectly then others can too so
be aware !

" DEDUCTION "

There will come a point in your life when
you will realise that you won't be able to
work along, one must have a group or a
team in order to work his/her way up

In the real world, as if you are in the reel
world you won't have to worry about these
thing because you are already working for
the real world people and so let's just focus
on the real world

For them the rules are quite strict
These companies aren't so simple,

Everything is complex on every level
Who doesn't wants the best, everyone does
but

Still their motto is .....

" Modest won't let you go anywhere
in life ! "

Which is true in a way
It's hypothetical to be honest !

And so in order to increase one must have
Many workers but they must be deduced/
subtracted at every level so that only the
best of the best survive, the competition
for the first floor is so high that when they
achieve it they will realise they don't
really control everything, there will
always be someone above them, which is in
every-case

" no matter who you are, the thirst
for power will never let you stop,
this journey won't end, there will
always be some thing else which will
make you crave to move forward
and to grab that victory or if you
don't want to win then someone will
make you move forward, you won't
control everything, Ever, it's the
only beauty of this process, that no
matter how hard you try, ...

humans will always find a way to do
the unexpected ! "

It's like the when you stack all those cards
just to reach the top and to realise that no
matter how hard you try if one falls, it will
make everyone fall and if everyone falls
then there is no way that you will be saved
in any case you will have to eventually
learn to take everyone with you or you
won't survive the Test Of Destiny

you will Expect the expected thinking It of
being unexpected but as the name the
unexpected is usually something which
you won't be able to think of that is why
future beholds the answers and they shall
never be seen before time or else those
answers will change and it will still result
in the unexpected !

'There is no running from the future "you'
are the future" and you have it now and so
you must save it before you see it slip like
grains of the sand from your hand which
you knew in advance you could have saved
them but you didn't because that one
moment of weakness made you slip aware
from the reality and so now you will
always be stuck in the reel world.

HAVE YOU
CREATED
YOUR OWN
BARS ?

Have you created your own bars ?
Not yet ?
Or maybe you have
You Just don't realise it yet !

The CRYZ1S are much better than you in
this topic you know their every move still
you don't learn from them,

Why is everyone PARANOID up there ?

May Because they know they should be !
It is as simple as that !

Don't complicate things ! :)

You are your own enemy !

You tag people in real life with labels
them being talkative or too much for me or
with name But
The point is don't just see people and their
tags which you have made those tags may
be a part of their personalities
But
You must Notice their behaviour too !
From which you will actually Learn

you won't Learn anything if you will
just go with their Appearance or
of what you think of them !

" Don't see them as humans
see them as books,
for every book
is capable of
teaching
you something !
which will be really
useful to you, only
if you will ask
the right questions
and that too
only if you will allow
yourself to see
the answers,
by looking
beyond your ego
allowing yourself
to realise
that no matter
how much you know
it still wont be enough ever
and so you must Keep Learning ! "

Now go the page 64 again
and observe it again
Not To read this time but to find an image,
Look it and then decide

What does it looks like ?

To some it will look like a
A piece from chess
Maybe an elephant, some will say a pawn,
A queen, a king or nowadays every figure
is weird in chess but look and decide what
do you see fix your answer and we shall
discuss it in the next page pg 66

What you see other's won't
Lets see if you are any different from the
others or you too just pretend to be,
And If am able to guess the right thing
About you or not !

Well I am sure
no matter which ever chess piece you
choose
I will guess it right !

And the answer will
surprise you !

" There is only one rule
you have to stick to one answer
Then only turn to the next page ..... "

It was never a chess participant
Or a chess piece
They do play they game by being in it
But The the real game is always between
the players !

Those who never show up in the chess
board because they are not allowed there
Only participants/pieces such things can
be there to perform {yes objectified} :|

If you thought of a chess piece
They obviously you lost
But if you did guessed the right answer
then you were able to look at the essence
of this book {yes that inVisible Essence }

The point is that no matter what
for most of you there was no chance by
which anyone would have won
because
I didn't gave you one !

You were shown a choice to choose form
but you were not aware of any other
choices you had,
and so like everyone
you got tricked into thinking
that the answer would be something
from the given choices

{it's never the case }

66

Even if you loose,
Don't get offended
But Understand !

Anyone who makes the game
will always have a purpose
to keep the victory for himself/herself
or if it was too easy then
Everyone would have won and
then the meaning of victory would have
defied its own meaning,
of whining alone !

The point is that no matter what you
choose it will always be 'Designed For You
To Loose', So don't look at the choices
You have now !
Look from a different perspective !
And try to find out a different option
The one which has not been given to you
yet

" To pass you must not rely on the
option which have been given to you,
creating one may create chaos and
so you must find the option which
has been kept hiding or the one
which already exist but you aren't
able to see it yet, try to find it and
you may get the victory "

What have you learned
from this chapter
?

To sum up
some will say
they have learned to lie,
for some it would be some information
they wanted,
for some it would be the knowledge
But

What do you see ?

Do you see the real answers
or are you still living a dream ?

The aim of this book was to make you
aware of how you are wasting your time,
The first page remember,
And so this answer was there but you
overlooked it, if you didn't then great,
But if you did then
Learn to observe proper
As I said .....

" Don't just read
But understand "

CH 4 IMPRESSION : THE EYE CANDY

Chocolate, toffee everywhere,
still no where to look for,
in my mind I have a world,
And everyplace to look for,
But still there is something missing...
Which I will never look for !

I know it doesn't rhyme well
The point is
It doesn't have to
Right ?
You don't watch the xyz show
because of logic,
Neither do you watch it
Because it has a awesome storyline

You watch it for eye candies !

Long gone the time when any show or
something had real sense or was without
any agenda, name one show or something
without a scandal or a boycott logo
attached, if they won't offend someone
maybe they wont be able to eat or maybe
this world will come to an end,

What's the point of life if you don't offend
someone ?
Right ?

60"

" long gone the time
for logic
when No Logic Rules
Over Logic
then There Is Something
Wrong
With The Audience
more
than the creators ! "

What do you do all day ?
What do you watch ?
Make a list of last 10 shows you have
watched !

I m not just saying this, do it !

And tell me if anyone of them
taught you something except violence,
and all the bad stuff in the world

Anyone one ?

No one !

" Easy to rule the world which is
divided and is consumed in their
own family matters "

Not everything is bad,
A coin always has two sides,
If used wisely you can purchase food from
that coin or get drunk and destroy your
life, with your own will, you have the
choice, the power, to make it stop,

TO MAKE AMENDS !

What is it that you are looking for ?
What is it that you are waiting for ?

The fruit which looks ripe from the outside
may be damaged from the inside !

You never know what's on the other side
Of what you see
Of what your perception is limited to !

Why it is Limited ?

So that you don't see,
The side which is not to be seen by you
Or else your faith, your trust would break
And then you will become loyal to yourself,
You will see and believe what you want to
Which clearly you as well as they don't
want !

Yes 'you', too don't want that !

But Why ?

Because everyone is scared
of facing the unpredictable
or the unknown

But at what cost ?

At the cost of being flocked around !

What is this fear which holds you,
stops you from being you ?

Why do you give yourself to this fear
Everyday knowing what you are doing
To yourself
Still you do it !

Why ?

Maybe because you want to do it
that's why ! ! !

A part of you will never let you go free ! ! !

It will always be there to hold you back !

Why are you holding yourself back
What is that fear which stops you
From leaving the dark side
In you ?
Why not let yourself free ?
When you know you have that power to be
free !

THE POSSIBILITY

You don't like these possibilities
You don't like getting burdened
by this pressure of making the right
choices !

Neither they like these possibilities
this Sense of Randomness
Even In The Known

You see what's so fascinating about the
future ?

That it can't be predicted
Even if you do predict it
There is a possibility that even what you
saw will Change
This is the beauty
The surprise element of this nature
Which is in it's nature
To change !

To evolve even if you don't want to, you
will have to change, you will be forced to !

When you know the change is coming
And you still can't do anything about it
Then there it makes no sense to go and see
everything in advance
Because since you can't change something
coming back
But

You won't be able to change other things
around that particular change which will
change !

Just like a stack of cards everything is
connect Believe It or not !

Your single move can either be the cause
of something bad or it can result in saving
the world

You change the world as you breathe in it
and you will , even if you won't

Change is all around you

It's happening right now !

As every second passes by
The world keeps on moving
Whether someone lives or dies

It was never about just you or me
Or even the humanity
There are a lot of other species on earth
As well, whose existence
you ignore everyday
And similarly they ignore yours
We accept a new theory as soon as it is
proven for us we are still considering
Possibilities
But at the same time ......

We want them to be accurate knowing that
even there is a possibility that whatever
we know is nothing, compared to even the
previous generations who existed on the
earth years ago ......

" The possibility
Not only contains your will
/human will
But other species will's also
It may contain
you being superior
and
not at the same time
It will also contain the death
and maybe the forgotten
concept of immortality
The new and old exists
together in now
But
in the possibility,
they would have never even existed
they could have been someone's
imagination as well as
a though or even a merged
consciousness
waiting for us just to get awake,

But the most important of all
It also contains
the possibility of loosing
Either the game
or
whatever we have right now,
And no one wants to loose
So why not
we can just consider
everyone who
thinks of
the possibility being real
as flawed
just so that
we can live the way we are living
without questioning anything
or without trying to change
anything ! "

If that's what you want
even that's a possibility
that the possibility
will give you that !

" THE HIDEOUT "

This is your hide out from the reality that
is why you go to this reel world,
So that you won't have to face the real you

Accept it !

Everyone does that !

If this reel world is not your hideout
Then something or maybe someone else
would be !

Maybe you haven't even noticed it yet or
it's just that you know it
but you don't want to accept it

because believing in something
which is not real makes you/ helps you
believe your own lies,

" What you think
Is merely what you want to think ! "

And to keep it that way
Your own mind will trick you !

To such an extent that until you believe it,
It Won't Stop !

Now when you know what your own mind
does to yourself,
now .....

Think what others are capable of doing
knowing this power that you have
without having the ability to control it
yourself ?
And to what extent ?

What does that mean ?

" It means that Is your hideout,

Really yours ?

Or is it a created one / designed

Just for you ? "

The chilling place,
your comfort zone,
your favourite shows,
those eye candies,
that zone you liked,
is it really your own zone,
What does it teaches you,
Forget about you,
What does it teaches your brain,
Your subconscious ?

Won't your brain
get more ideas watching those things you
want to see for your entertainment,
Your brain will learn
from those things you watch
and will improvise
and will try to make you believe
the lies which your brain has specifically
created for you
because what your brain is really trying to
do here is that it is
Trying to save ? you ?
From seeing the real you ?

Have you seen yourself in the mirror ?
What do you see ?

Do you see yourself ?

Or

Do you see a reflection ?

Another copy

Of a copy which was being sold too you ?

Do you really see "YOU" ?

But evolution happens
Everything could turn right
If possible

But this won't happen
Because this is what you think !

Your brain is trying to convince you
That everything will be alright

Keep going the way you are going
Keep going to that HIDEOUT

See those eye candies
Watch those shows

"Yes",
Evolution will happen but this is how it is
going to happened if you won't take
control of yourself .....

" Then they would loose their
Own identity
In the fear of loosing their mask "

Some genius would say isn't it good
If the mask takes over ?

To that genius I would say
You don't need to think is it good or bad
because yours has already taken over ! ! !

Go to mirror and check genius
You will find yourself
But not yourself in that mirror

" Maybe you lost the real you
When you thought of doubting
yourself "

Of making yourself believe
that the reel world is real
and the real isn't,

That day you lost it when
You gave up the fight,

The fight to take yourself back from that
deep pit of Infinity,

From that Pool of temptations,
Which won't let you out at any cost

because it survive till you are in it
When you will leave it will die
It will not prosper !

Your hope genius which was destroyed
That made you weak !

Your lust, your fears of facing the reality
That made you weak !

It made you so weak
That you started to think that giving up to
these temptations, watching this or that is
cool it's the new strong, but it isn't ! ! !

Being weak is never being strong

Strong are those
who won't give up
Who won't listen
to even themselves
To stand for what's right!

They wont give in
to these temptations
like what you did genius !

You fight is not
with someone else
But with your own

If you control yourself
You will rule
your own world

But

If you don't
Then you will become a puppet
For some else

And

They will control you
if you won't control yourself !

But

You will never loose
If you won't give up
If you face those fears
That reality
That truth to accept the real you
And if you are daring enough
To come out of that imagination

Then

And only then
Will you be able to see above yourself
And will see even those who are trying to
play with you !

But until that time comes
Believe in yourself !
Keep trusting yourself
No matter what
you will come out of it one day !

With this faith in yourself
You will be shown a way out,

" Just trust and go
where your heart takes you,
where the truth takes you and
Where the real you takes you ! "

CH 5 PARTY WITH COOKIES

THE COOKIE PREDICTS

YOU HAVE NO IDEA
WHAT YOU HAVE SIGNED UP FOR !

Cookies are homemade
They are FREE !!!
There are of different types
Some would like your name
Some would like your like you email
Some would even like your bank account
details and where you spend your money

Have fun eating and storing them !

Every person In problem
Will always ask the bad guy
why ?

Why are you doing this ?

isn't it obvious

he/she is the bad guy
Come on use your brain !
The bad guy in this stupid movie will care
so much to explain that I was your enemy
form long your family has done this and
that to me

" No "

What are you people dreaming ?

These things may happen
in the real world
but in the reel world
this would happen.....

The bad guy acts deaf
And will never reply
Taking your data along
he/she will live his life

Why ?

Because you accepted to take that cookie !
didn't you ?

You accepted ? You gave your consent ?

It will never work
If you won't let it
But in some cases it won't matter
if you give your consent or not
Thats also true

So what exactly is the cookie game ?

A game of theft ?

Mostly it's about your data
Being served,

But sometimes
They won't show a cookie
Some weird sound
will be produced
as soon as you open a page
or something

A stupid pop up
Saying
Your phone has been infected
Download this to protect yourself
'No', don't do that

wasn't it obvious in the first place when
you go out to hunt a prey
someone will always be there
who will consider you as his/her prey ?

Why am I using her,
You should never underestimate !
Everyone is a genius sitting next to you
now a days,
I don't get it when people try to think they
rule the world because they are are at the
top, but the truth is someone rules them
too. Always ! :)
What happens after they consider you as
their prey the same thing which happened
when you consider someone as your prey,
you go for a hunt, plant a trap and
then wait,
just for the right time,
until either they get trapped or
either you give up

This is a long game
Result are usually in the favour of
The person
who hunts

Because all he/she has to do
is to wait for your one wrong move,
To wait for you to take a step ahead,
And even if you won't get caught
Someone will !

Everyone's a genius now a days
remember ?

Some geniuses would hunt
other will get trapped,
but this legacy of geniuses will go on.....

Speaking of traps .....
Do cookies remind you of any other thing
Which is similar to them

Just think you know about them
You even get trapped in them
Everyday

Even I do get trapped in them
somedays

But then on the other days
when I stop caring
it just won't affect
Or distract me
of my precious time
Any guess
Here it is .....

{ next page }

(◎)
LOADING

10 LIKES on your photo
from strangers

SEND BIRTHDAY WISH
To your uncle's dog !

Say hi to Xyz whos new here
& Doesn't care about you !

Message (by
The Most Intellectual Person
who is promoting not to use phone
by using his phone) :
Probability of you
getting Scammed into
every stupid notification
is much higher than
you actually getting
the content you deserve !

" The Scam of Personalised
Notifications "

Hey you just got a message !

from abc
When checked and downloaded that app
to see the message
It turns out it was a message
send by THE BOT
saying your abc friend
has just jointed say hi to him/her !
Turns out they made a
fool out of that person,
Wasted the data we had
just so that they could force us into
downloading this app
Anger us deletes the app
And next time
Next month
Download it again
Just to find out that it was a scam
A.gain !
Then even after 2 months we will
download again thinking
what if he/she really send me a text,
just to realise
their BOT iS in love with you
so much
that it Won't Stop
spamming you !

Another one similar is

" The For You Section "

This section is everywhere
in literally everything !

They don't even let
you shop groceries freely,
even there will be a for you section,
Maybe they just forgot that we are humans
with consciousness
and we don't want to be guided,
I have purchased dry fruits last winter
and but it will recommend it in summers
maybe I don't want dry fruits in summers

but the for you section,
Just replicates your behaviour
If you are thinking AI is Intelligent

It's not !

It may work in some things very
accurately
but fails to work in another

One can say it totally depends from
company to company
Which is true !

But

Still have you every imagined
if it is for us

The FOR YOU section
then why still it doesn't match our
expectations ?

Maybe
because even if they know what
you want
they won't give it to you that easy,
this could be a strategy,

I have notice it, just when I am about to
leave the app after getting annoyed,
there comes something relatable
and more accurate,
Just when I am about to give up,
There comes my saviour,
It could be a strategy,

Don't Underestimate
The AI !!!

you never know
if you were wrong
all along and they knew it,
just so that you could spend some
More some extra time
finding the real things
you really want to find,

maybe also because
you know that
they are the best in the market
and the will provide us with the
information we want,
maybe we have to
just keep searching,
with this information in mind
we would continue to search
saving ourselves from the
BLACKHOLES of the internet world
THE ECHO CHAMBERS in CH 6
we would make it to the video we want to
see if we pass these tests,
because these echo chambers
are infinite just like our curiosity
they trap us with our own will,
just so that we don't go away,
with all the attention they could grab,
building the suspense,
with the power of fantasy
they hold the consumer,
just like a bee trapped
Inside the spider web,
it could buzz but it won't move,

"yes",
the more they create buzz
the more they are trapped
and the closer they get to their death
because the spider will eventually come to
that bee to eat it

Think about it in this way suppose you
watched some video,
you write about it in the comments how
stupid this video was,
you write about it's stupidity
on other platforms too,
it gives that video a shoutout in a bad way
but since

" any kind of publicity is good
publicity "

People will go and watch that video and
will waste their time just to know what
you were talking about,

if you think you wasted other people's
time, it's not that simple
you wasted your own time too,
you could have just left that page
but you didn't,
you stopped there
to write bad things about that video
there you wasted your time,
then you did the same thing again
by trying destroying that persons image
on other platforms,
that persons image won't get destroyed
obviously,
but by this behaviour he/she will get
famous,

you have wasted your time well enough,
by now but then some abc supporter of
that person will definitely comment on
your stuff, then again
You will fight with them also,

and so a simply act of ignorance could
have saved you one or two hours of your
day, but what happened ?

Your ego wasn't satisfied ! isn't ?

And so you continued.....
Like always !

And so did everyone
no one just stops,

Look around you , no seriously LOOK ! :)

Go notice their behaviour

See what people are doing !

Don't rush to comment
but just observe !

And you will find out
how this stupidity won't end,

it will go on and on .....

97

Just like a discussion
which is meant to be stretched !

And which platform won't like such a raise
in their new users,
just to add some oil
they will review something out of
nowhere,
Just to create this buzz and
reopen that closed
or forgotten topic again,

You think you are fighting ?

That You are on one side ?

'No', they are making you fight !
Even by letting you fight !

Those terms and conditions
you just signed
with a click
also meant they have
the right over the content
and if they find it offensive
they will remove it,

it should be done, it's right

but for both the sides !

But they won't do it for both the sides
EVER !

Because then the fight might end
and who in the world doesn't like negative
publicity

which will make their platform just so
suitable to fight,

So before even you think to fight

Use your brain and think

" Is this really your fight ? "

can't everyone just have peace ?

Who is bigger the one who fights
or the one who forgives ?

But if you still choose to fight

Maybe you will win the conversation
You were fighting over

But

You will surely loose all that
Time
which was worth
Doing something useful !

Think and choose wisely !

CH 6 ECHO CHAMBER

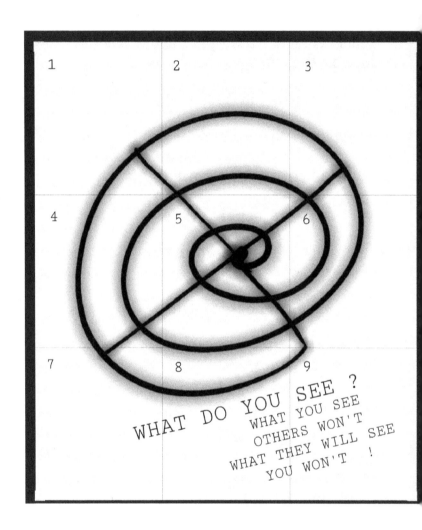

WHAT DO YOU SEE ?
WHAT YOU SEE
OTHERS WON'T
WHAT THEY WILL SEE
YOU WON'T !

The much awaited topic is here ! ! !
Clap audience
Let everyone hear the sound of your
applause .....
Even if no one claps you will still hear the
sound
Everything is usually pre recorded with
sound effects which were not even
produced in the real life

What actually happens when you watch a
comedy show and if no one laughs,
probably you won't even laugh,
but since you hear a pre recorded sound of
people laughing your brain tells you to
laugh, it signal you to laugh,
It replicates their behaviour, just like
monkeys do when they see a human, brain
is a monkey, said in so many books, even
in spiritual books, and it is true, my
respects to that thinking,

But we will talk a step ahead to
understand this carefully,
your brain likes to replicate
what it sees or what it hears
or feels with the senses

Right ok ?

You with me ?

Now when you see a comedy show you listen to the jokes with your conscious mind, and if you are really well focused waiting for the show anchor to crack a joke, listening carefully, consciously then your sub conscious will react to that laughing sound when the audience laughs, by creating a mood or a will in you to laugh,

similarly,
When your subconscious sees something or listens to something which is not happening in front of your conscious brain but in-front of your subconscious Brain it will want to see that
A.gain !

It is human behaviour to get influenced
You can't just get out of the league and say
I won't be influenced,

because you will be accept it or not,

So how is this Echo chamber exactly designed ?

From what I have seen and understood

It is made of many components
One of the main factor being .....

" SIMILARITY "

[it may Includes the following
but surely is not limited to only them] :)

* Sub Conscious Messaging *

including sub conscious messaging,
not the conspiracy one but subconscious
messaging in the sense
that if you see something with a
subconscious message they will
recommend other similar things,
AI is not human,
what it does is it REPLICATES,
for example a video had laughing sound in
it's background and your watch time of
that video was high then it will
recommend you other videos with same or
similar laughing sound and its just not
limited to sound
but
What we consider subconscious
or not to be seen by our conscious it can
Also be same for the things which are seen
by the conscious, another example could
be you watched a video with a pink
background it may recommended you a
video with a similar background,
the things which are subconscious for you
are not for the AI,

from the AI's perspective those things are
the common patterns,
Until it Learns about you,
very fast solely by itself, it will take some
time for the AI to predict you,
seeing the technology grow at a rapid
speed that time won't be long enough,
it will come Soon!

* Conscious *

It may also recommend the similar
content which one may find is related to
him/her how he/she thinks
for example if you watch videos of a
particular political party, you will always
be shown their side and not the other side,
if someone knows what you like and what
you want to see, it becomes easy to keep
you on their platform, no one does this on
purpose but it's done so that they reach
their daily target time which they should
obtain from you, in other words your daily
average of using their product.

* Other Patterns *

They many also consider other new
patterns, they may be related to a person,
what type pf a person watch what type of

content, to sort everything they must
divide everyone in different categories,
I wonder which category I might be in ?
Hmm tough one ? Not really !
Everything is easy for the AI
Everything goes through a process,
since every specification is tailored by a
human just like command being given in
the right directions,
those orders will definitely result in
producing the kind of product they want,

For e.g.

Group wise :   very intelligent
                                  {But with low income}

Behaviour can be predicted :

                                    these people
                              are usually angry

Everything is predictable see ?

Okay ! Fine !

Maybe not everything !

special not

HUMAN BEHAVIOUR !

So it still doesn't matter how many
complex degrees you have
you will not be able to decode
every single thing,

You forgot you made the AI
Humans made the best Computers
No matter how best those computers be
In what they do
They can beat humans in chess
But not in real life
If it's not reel then
there will be a chance for you to win ?

You can compete
but can't
Predict those who
don't even know how they feel
They may be able to tell
With the
SYNTHETIC EMOTIONS they have
But
They won't ever be 100% accurate !

Even people with real emotion
can't tell exactly what the
other person is thinking or is feeling
isn't ?

Everything you see today
Has been made by someone else
And you are on your own journey to create
something useful for everyone right ?

But all the things made by humans
Not ever human is good
at working or making use of those things

But with AI , they could with their power
of memorising and humans being creative
maybe they could pave the future,

Make a better world ?

Who knows what the future beholds !

* A Particular Brand *

Suppose if someone likes to watch videos
from a particular brand account
or they follow someone blindly or trust
them completely, then those ads
companies might even compete
to get their ad on that brand,
you know why ?
Because of you !
Where you are !
The Profit is !

And so a particular brand which keeps you
consumed every time you open the net
you will be shown some of their content so
that your royalty won't move even if they
won't upload the new thing they will show
you their older posts,

because then, those ads by which their companies earn may advertise many times in a year { there are many companies by the way } but the goal is not just to advertise but it is also to keep you hooked, tuned in, so that when the time comes you will show up just like a trusted person will, so at that moment they will take their profits at double by throwing every possible thing they can at you to recover the money the didn't earned a previous month or any loss they experienced due to someone being inactive for a long time.

* Category *

They also like to recommend on the basis of what category you like the most to watch comedy, signing, etc
but these categories are not limited they are also divide by the AI for e.g. these video are not only the kid videos but the ice-cream ones, or the ones with expensive futuristic toys, even if you don't mention every single detail it would be detected and will be shown accordingly,
everything is sorted
in some tables or triangles
in the the reel world,
for them it's really easy to manipulate even those who deserted them and moved to another space,

if they start focusing on every single one,
but as you know they don't care,
because with the increase in population
there is an increase in demand,
and where the demand is
not only platforms flourish but workers
also start competing in order to get what
they want,

what exactly does everyone wants ?

A sense of security with no ups and downs
but then why is it so that someone not
offering that has so many people working
for them ?

Because they no where the future is, ?
moreover ......

" in business there is
no place for ego !
one needs another
and vice versa. "

* According to your Gender *

A particular gender will be interested in a
particular gender,
now the world is changing ;)

being more accepting and so your
demands will be fulfilled just with a simple
search your pattern will be observed,
even the AI can now tell who do you like
and who you don't,
but you won't tell that to yourselves,
simply because you are being a regular
human this is what we do, the unusual !

* According to your Age *

What your age group likes you may like it
but this is not always the case, your age in
the reel world will be determined by your
IQ level, either you are intellectual or not,
are your preferences like old people do you
like to watch news or are you young you
watch updates you see someone can love
updates too and so
for the AI it's not your real age which will
select your recommendations it will be
your MENTAL AGE !!!

* The Colour you like *

Colours tell a lot,
it speak in itself
like
purple can depict richness
or red can make you angry,
white can pacify things

Colour can be used even to fuel an agenda
or distinguish it but AI doesn't work like
that ! Humans does,
an AI will simply detect the usual colour
you watch, is it a pink background, pink
shirt, pink curtains, also it's not limited to
that maybe they will find your colours
purchasing pattern and recommend you
videos with that particular coloured
product.

* Date Of Birth *

Your date categories you in another
category it tell about your thinking
the same age group thinks a lot alike
however
they will be always a few to be the
difference from the group but mostly they
all can be grouped and are thus are
predictable,
those new short terms that your parents
won't know the meaning of
you would because you are from the new
generation and
what you like will surely determine the
future for technology and so you must like
the old videos too,
because if you will only like the newer
content then what about the previous one,
watch time will get decreased and .....

So in order to make you like
you will be shown that one stupid video
which you hate and dislike
which shows up on your page forever even
if you don't want it to show up,
it will until you start liking it,
I bet this has happened to you !
isn't ?

How do I know it ?

Because I have experienced it too but then
why you weren't able to notice it ?

Because you didn't cared too,

" you were just thinking that you are
going with the flow not knowing
that, that flow was predicted !!! "

But now some genius will ask it doesn't
make sense seeing a video again and again
in feed how will they change my opinion ?
This is stupid ! 'No', its not !
No one will change your opinion,
only you can do that,

See this is the beauty of this process
That you are in Control !
but the Real Question is
FOR HOW LONG ?

Familiarity ends Fear !

and so does it develops liking,
watching something again and again will
make you familiar to that concept
and you will eventually start liking that
concept even if you didn't liked it in the
start,
There will be a few things which in text
will make us awe and keep us in a state of
being impressed by the ones who help
created this process
but somewhere in your heart,
even in their heart
they will know
it's a mess they have created
and know they are surely not the ones who
can control it all by themselves at-least !

* Language Analysis *

Nice name ! Wow you look so good today !
Have you ever seen someone being polite
on the internet
except for the verified id's ?

Ever ?

'No' !

Because people have become so familiar to
the net that they have started showing
their real sides

" forgetting that once the thing is on
the net it will live there forever",

Back in the old days, when people had no
internet,
only in bad circumstances will people get
forced to show their true colours
but now a days it not that difficult to see
someone,
sure it is in the real life but not in the reel
life,

" In The Reel Life they roam free,
thinking They Are free
while Being Monitored all the time ",

even if you weren't properly able to define
Irony at least now you exactly what it is !

* Feel Good Vibes *

Oh don't even start with these,
feel good videos
are much different than motivation
they don't want you to get motivated ! , ...

or else you will leave,
feel good videos are those videos with
people in those who make it look like
that they know everything,
they try to find a problem in your question
and when
the real question will come
they will just puzzle you
and end the topic,
just when you will get so frustrated that
your doze didn't worked, what you have
watched your taste has been compromised
you will eventually watch another video to
cover it up,
just like an alcoholic will do if they ate
something suppose say tasty with their
bad stuff ,
the last thing they will put in their mouth
will not be those cashews but it will be that
drink they hate.
You meet the person before you leave
them,
because
if you will go without meeting them you
will come back just to see them, it's
different if you love them, then surely you
will come back whether you see them
before you leave or not.
And so an addict
will always
be loyal to his drink
than his Kind.

THE SECRET RECIPE

TELL THEM WHAT THEY WANT TO HEAR!

TRAGET them on a personal level !

YOU ARE LOOKING GOOD TODAY TELL US WHAT'S NEW ?

Am I ?

USE THEIR FEARS !

" THE SECRET "

What will happen if only you
know the secret
will keep it to yourself ?
It will remain a secret and will never come
out because the only possibility won't even
be possible you wont tell that to anyone !
you are not that stupid, are you ?
No one is !
But
if you tell your secret to anyone,
it will be mainly to acquire/gain their trust
in you In Order to tell them that
you are so true to them that you won't
ever lie to them,
Right ?
But chances to that secret getting leaked is
also really low because then it will become
obvious that the only person who knew
your secret spilled it out,
The person responsible for leaking out
your secret could still be found if you tell
that secret to even a large number of
people,

" Everything is Traceable ",

but you will only trace this much if that
secret meant a lot to you,
Right ?
But .....

"In the reel world
you may find a lot of secrets,
openly kept,
just there for everyone to see them",

weird right ?

why would they keep their secrets
exposed ?

because they don't care !

it is either :

1 because they know that you won't be
able to do anything about it or

2 because of the fact that they know you
won't do anything

That is

1 Means that even if you protest it
It wont be enough to take them down

and

2 means that you will support them
eventually,

which everyone does clearly !

There is a serious need
of some serious Laws
with no boundaries
and everyone will have to follow them a
safe digital space for everyone ! ?

Where maybe we can teach the AI some
good stuff , block the posts automatically i
am not just taking about keywords but
about pictures and about the other things.

What if AI was
smart enough
even to decode
the difference between
what's being said
and
what's the hidden message, is it ?
between
what is being portrayed
and what is being
kept hidden
even in the written form !

" The biggest secrets are not
hidden, because there is
no need to hide them
since we live in them !!! "

CH 7 THE PENETRABLE
LEAKAGE

DATA-DATA
EVERYWHERE
NOWHERE TO GO
AND
NOWHERE TO HIDE
CZ YOUR TRACES
ARE ALL OVER
THE WEB
AND EVEN IN
YOUR
FAVOURITE
INCOGNITO SITE

Some sites may crash
They say
If you block all the cookies
from your device

" And literally
Every single site won't work "

It you block every cookies
There is a option you can do that

But you won't be able to use
any site then

It turns out that

" The term Free isn't so free ? "

It lost it's freedom long ago
Joke ?

Maybe not !

There is
no use of even the precious DATA
Which is being collected if one doesn't
knows

How to use it !

Right ?

DATA

is everywhere it's being produced
more massively then ever before
every micro second somewhere data is
being produced and stored and going all
into heavy processing
through which
will comes those results
which would then determine the way
In which
Everything will take place,
like literally !

You can control control a flock of sheeps

but

what you can't do is to fully control
numerous flock of sheeps
just growing everyday !

you can monitor them !

but to what extent ?

and who will decide what's right
and what's wrong ?

And

Here comes the new concept
Of .....

" THE DATA OVERFLOW "

A thing which no one will accept, ! ! ! ! ! !

Imagine the power of being in control
to able to control the thing you want
to the way you want, long gone that days,
When
the number of workers working was only
3% of the complete whole, ?
then at what extent can you monitor,
AI and bots can do some good work but
they are not accurate,
at-least not yet ?
maybe in they future they will be !
who knows ?

When things get out of control
Then even the rulers won't be able to
rule the kingdom they have created
Everything will go in the hand of the
destiny, fate
and it will create a new merit for
everyone,
But there is always a but
and that is a creator never abandons his/
her creation be it a scientist or a gardener
everyone plays an important role
and they will try their best to save those
crops from being eaten by the rodent as
well as by those harmful pesticide,
but will it be too late by then ?

" THE <u>future</u> beholds
all the answers
yet it is so
UNCERTAIN ! "

Anything can happen
in just
The blink of an eye;)
even something which
you would have never even imagined !

what's the buzz now ?
It
may never be there in the first place
and everything can even change
with some miscellaneous efforts

if not kept well treated
those crop may never even flourish in the
first place !

The creators
monitor everything
for the good of everyone,
At least this is what they think
they are doing
who doesn't want peace and longitivtiy ?

Right ?

But

There are people ready
with their schemes,
frauds, scams, its all in-front of you,
waiting

..... LOADing .....

just for the right opportunity,
for the right moment,
for the right time,
for you to get caught,
be aware
of Your surroundings,
it's better to be paranoid these days !

Since everyone will shift to their
New digital life { Coming soon ; LAME ? }

Life wont be that easy !

Unless you learn to :)

Adjust

And

Adapt

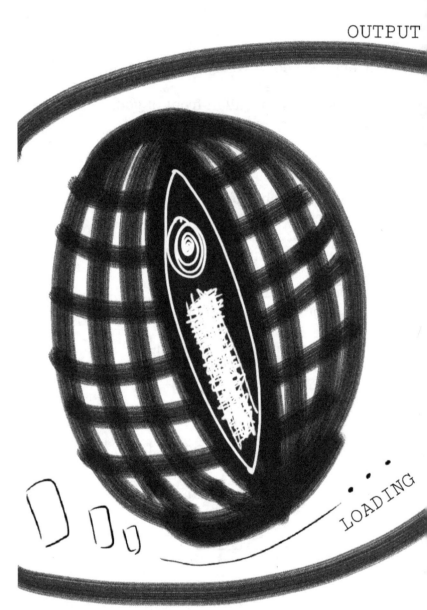

LOADING

INPUT (DATA + CATCH)

A
MONITOR
CAN BE
USED TO MONITOR
AS WELL AS
TO BE MONITORED !

An eye
can now roam in the entire world without
being noticed and even without being seen,

What comes with that free stupid stuff
which you Just downloaded,
you don't know,

Speaking of free
those catch are not just there to rot,
that extra data you didn't used
but it got locked,
is not just there
responsible for you having less storage,
every mail waiting
for your just one click
is not made with a thinking that you will
decode them,

Everyone plays just to win,
Everyone has their own chance
but those people defiantly
have an upper-side
from those who knows nothing,
Which is everyone ! Literally !

What you are being prepared for ?
you don't know yet !
that scam call might seem so realistic
but as you will download the said
who knows maybe your phone will get
mirrored, everything comes with a cost,

" a cost which you will have to pay
for not being aware ! "

And if you think
you are in control

Then you are wrong !

There is no such thing as

" I.m.penetrable "

*Surprise

Everything, everyone has their own
weaknesses, things don't usually have
them but sometimes they have been
created that way on purpose with a
weakness in case something goes wrong
so they will be able to use that weaknesses
as their strength
and will do the right thing
which is needed to be done !

Surprise*

You can't stop
the water from flowing
Or the wind
from going to it's
Destination

Just like sand they will slip away
But by taking you with them
And you may never find any single grain
of sand responsible for it
being loose from your hand
being the cause
of the whole sand getting slipped away,

But sometimes
Even in the animal kingdom
The prey may find
the predator just to slip away
Or sometimes
The predator
will leave the prey when it's
being no fun to them
Call it luck
or chance
but you knew
you did that on purpose,

" Find a purpose
before getting lost in this world,
or else you may find yourself in
these stupid games ! "

CH 8 FORCE AND MATTER ;
BEING INSEPARABLE

" YOU ARE NOT APART
FROM THIS SYSTEM
YOU ARE A PART OF THIS SYSTEM
AND THE MORE YOU
DENY IT
THEN MORE YOU DEFEND IT
AND YOU KNOW IT
BUT YOU JUST WONT ACCPET IT
BECAUSE NOW IT'S EXISTENCE
RAISES A QUESTION ON YOURS
AND AS SOON AS
EVEN ANYONE WILL
THINK TO SNATCH IT WAY
YOUR SURVIVAL INSTINCTS WOULD
JUMP IN
THEY WILL DEFEND IT TO SUCH AN
EXTINCT
JUST LIKE ANY ADDICT
WHO WILL DO
ANYTHING
FOR THAT SINGLE DROP
KNOWING
THAT IT WILL DESTROY HIM
BUT
KNOWING IS NOT ENOUGH
NOTHING EVER IS !!! "

Repeating Glitch ? Interesting ...... ;)

Some would read it ЄΙGHT,
To　　　　　some the number is
ΙΝFΙΝΙΤY,

But what I may tell you today,
It's not going to be pretty,
Your sheer ignorance
won't let you see
Your curiosity
won't let you leave
No matter what
you do today,
you will alway
live vulnerably !

You think
what you want is this
Wait for the next day
Your thinking will change
What you want is never-ending
"yes", your needs are never enough
Everyday is different
But same in the aspects of you
being the same you !

131

Despite doing emotional well,
despite having unique thinking and
even making sense forever,
There is something about you and me
Which will never change

Your situations can
But what won't change is
You and me being HUMANS
AND LET BE THAT WAY ONLY !

No matter what you do
Everything will just take you back
to one question
to your existence
Your long longing
for a purpose for which neither your
conscious nor your subconscious
will stop looking for
it will always try to find that purpose
which will make you
the better version of you,
you want to be,

" Our biggest strengths can also be
our biggest weaknesses "

And all you can do is to try
to control yourself with your will power
not only that is needed
but .....

You should be trained
so well enough to fight
those addictions that
that trap won't even let you
even think of leaving the real world
and going into the reels world ! {glitches ?
Will talk about it in next book}

But how will this happen ?
This can happen only and only if your
Needs are biG enough
to force you on the right path,
because if we look closely they are our
needs which makes us do
the things we are doing right now,
some situations may differ,
but those needs
push us to do something
which is above us
to do the right thing,
which is needed to be done !

" Let your heart wander
And you brain think
But those will always be your needs
Which will make you WIN/k "

*If you want to really win
then one must control his/her needs*

133

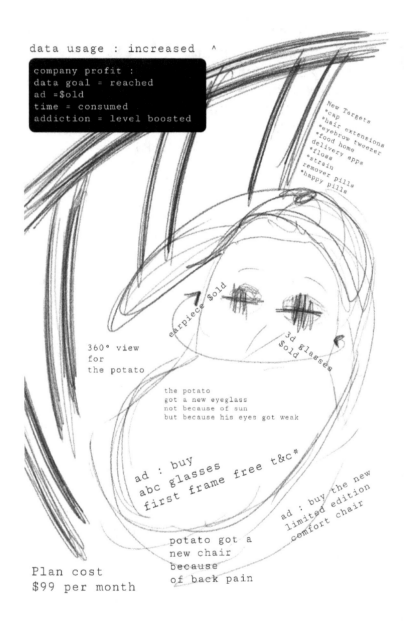

data usage : increased   ^

company profit :
data goal = reached
ad =$old
time = consumed
addiction = level boosted

New Targets
*cap
*hair extensions
*eyebrow tweezer
*food home
 delivery apps
*floss
*strain
 remover pills
*happy pills

earpiece $old

3d glasses
$old

360° view
for
the potato

the potato
got a new eyeglass
not because of sun
but because his eyes got weak

ad : buy
abc glasses
first frame free t&c*

ad : buy the new
limited edition
comfort chair

potato got a
new chair
because
of back pain

Plan cost
$99 per month

134

Every problem
every created
always has a solution
waiting for it to be used
at the right time and so as we discussed
above the needs we will talk about those in
the next chapter,
but firstly we will need too see the problem
more closely and so with all my respects to
everyone
Offending everyone's here I am

Introducing to you

"The POTATO"

Welcome to the future of us !!! ;)

The potato is innocent,
it may come in various sizes
it can be short or long, thin or health,
But
what is for certain is that it is to be sold,
Sorry we don't need the potato !
All we need is his/her TIME !
All that we can take !
Every possible possibility of it !

Potato also thinks that he/she has a choice
But just to refresh the potatoes memory
here is a game
Designed specially for potatoes .....

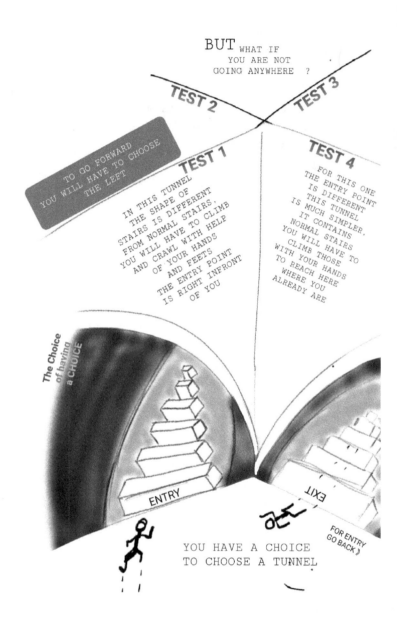

BUT WHAT IF
YOU ARE NOT
GOING ANYWHERE   ?

TEST 2

TEST 3

TO GO FORWARD
YOU WILL HAVE TO CHOOSE
THE LEFT

TEST 1

IN THIS TUNNEL
THE SHAPE OF
STAIRS IS DIFFERENT
FROM NORMAL STAIRS.
YOU WILL HAVE TO CLIMB
AND CRAWL WITH HELP
OF YOUR HANDS
AND FEETS
THE ENTRY POINT
IS RIGHT INFRONT
OF YOU

TEST 4

FOR THIS ONE
THE ENTRY POINT
IS DIFFERENT
THIS TUNNEL
IS MUCH SIMPLER.
IT CONTAINS
NORMAL STAIRS
YOU WILL HAVE TO
CLIMB THOSE
WITH YOUR HANDS
TO REACH HERE
WHERE YOU
ALREADY ARE

The Choice
of having
a CHOICE

ENTRY

EXIT

FOR ENTRY
GO BACK)

YOU HAVE A CHOICE
TO CHOOSE A TUNNEL

You might choose
a tunnel and start moving
just so that one day because you think you
will reach there
you will start trying
without even thinking
why I didn't had other choices
when I was making this decision !

Maybe a choice to quit and to choose from
what I want to choose from,
but that clearly wasn't the case
you will always be given a choice
but still it won't be near
of what you really want,
and if you want that choice
then you will have to create it yourself ! ?
There is no other way
This is how it works
Either you choose from the given options
and be dependable
Or you make your own game, ?
with your chosen choices from which
you can choose
but the cost of making this move will be big
because then there will be no turning back
and you will be on your own.
Alone !

*Also escaping a game just to create
another one ? Hmmm ...... really good
decision think about it ! *

You were on your own
even when you had a choice
it was just that
you saw what you wanted to see,
you just accepted the situations
as they were shown to you,
But now when you know
how to change

{ do you ? }

it's up to you ! ?

" For the change
to take place, You will have to
be the change yourself ! "
*Not by creating a new mess but
by thinking and staring from
what you have and
what you can do about it ! *

But
some genius will say
I will Still choose
which is most of you

{In real life when In real situations}

to them I will say .....

138

All I could see them do is that who's game
will they play from abc company or def
company forgetting the main point in the
first place
that why arre they even playing it
in the first play because they want to ?
Or is it because they have seen their
friends do so ?

Do you want to copy your friends
be their replicas ?
or do you idealise someone and want to be
like them, do what they are doing
in their life, have you ever thought that
why every face on the earth is so different
and unique ?

And even if their faces are similar
their behaviours aren't
why ?
Because they were born unique
to do something unique !

Don't copy anyone use your brain
Because what is special about you
is not about them and vice versa,
everyone has their own specialities don't
underestimate yourself,
you are the best !
Just believe in yourself !
And you will eventually
find your own new way ? or a hidden one !

CH 9 THE LEARNINGS ;
RETRIEVE AND REVIVE

```
   DON'T EXPECT
     TOO MUCH
YOU MIGHT GET UPSET
    BY KNOWING
   HOW MUCH YOU
    DON'T KNOW !
```

The main question is
Is there a possibility to RETRIEVE ?

CAN YOU REVIVE ?

What's lost is gone !

You can't bring back something
Or undo those things which you have
already done

But

You can make sure that you
Or anyone else don't repeat that mistakes

By making them aware !

By reminding yourself again and again of
What you are getting into
And what are the consequences
Which
You will have to face !

We are here today,
We may never get this chance tomorrow
So today must be yours
For you to keep
For your own use
And so
in this chapter
we are going to discuss .....

How you can prevent the time getting lost
from yourself
AGAIN ?

Never a.gain ! ! !

Ans =

Be Specific

It is the only thing which will save you
from you ! by stopping you from getting
drifted from your desired only,
Look for what you want
Don't roam in the jungle aimlessly or
The chances are you will
Get lost ! offended ? ;)

Use sounds

Sounds are the best, they are the product
of nature, and so the best sounds are the
ones which are also created by the nature
e.g water waves, all the sound you hear are
either converted or made digital to analog
blah blah but the point is nature's sounds
the most perfect try listening to that if you
can otherwise others will work too, but
will not be the best, because only those can
heal who created you,
i.e our mother nature

142

Keep a watch

On yourself as you go further you may lose
the time being mesmerised by how things
work but keep a limit for yourself to use
everything so that you don't exhaust
yourself.

Write it

Make a list of what you want and what are
you currently doing about it, follow your
own lead, notice and point out your
mistakes yourself that where you went
wrong and lost 3 hrs of your day,
keep a record of everything !

Leave

Learn to say 'no', to the things which don't
matter the most to you, dedicate your time
to the precious things so that you won't
have to regret them latter in life.

Form your own opinions

And you will be able to do that if you will think about the problem as a whole not in parts.

Alone time

You must $pend some time with yourself or you will forget yourself the real you, take some time from your busy schedule for yourself, doing nothing but for sitting idle for sometime with yourself for letting those ideas flow which will change you and your life too.

Set your Goals

You must have a goal before proceeding further or else you will get lost for sure, to maintain a rhythm you must work and to do that you must have some work and that work will be provided to you only if you want it with the help of your goals.

* Ask yourself : Is it worth ? *

It's all about the worth, are you worthy
enough to understand or to do something
about your life now ?
If you are
then do what your life has taught you,
not
what someone wants you to do,
do what's best for everyone
not what you think is best for you,
but
still believe in yourself
because
your heart may dishearten you
if you don't give in to those temptations,
stay focused
and work towards your goal,
and you will
realise
one day that
your life was

worth it !

As we move to the end .....
{AGED remember ?}

What do you THINK ?
You have your own reasons ?
Everyone does !

Everyone thinks that they are doing the
right thing which is needed to be done,

how is it even possible
that everyone is being right and wrong
at the same time ?

It's only possible in the real world ! ?

where these conflicts are raised to such an
Extinct
that people would fight
to prove their opinion

But

in the reel world,
every move has it's own consequences
not only the good people face them
but the bad ones too

Life is complex
on either side s ; be it
Reel or Real
Really is it ?

146

Everything is just so complicated
But
When you be in it
Face it,
try to be like Everyone,
you will understand that,

" to life the meaning is not just about
existence
about existing
but it is also about living it fully. "

so be who you, or try to be
but for you to be
you must live
by not just existing
but by living it.

May you live forever
Joke ? Maybe next time ......

Live :)

In harmony
By Default*

147

Youtube channel -	IT'S SIMPLE - Priyanka
Instagram id -	@itssimplepriyanka
Facebook page -	@itssimplepriyanka
Twitter -	@itssimplepri

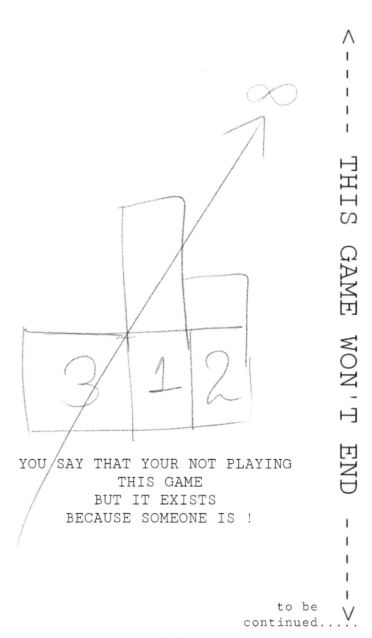

THIS GAME WON'T END

YOU SAY THAT YOUR NOT PLAYING
THIS GAME
BUT IT EXISTS
BECAUSE SOMEONE IS !

to be
continued.....